PRO-LIFE, PRO-CHOICE, PRO-LOVE

44 days of reflection for finding a third way in the abortion debate

Other Books in the Where True Love Is Series

Where True Love Is: an affirming devotional for LGBTQI+ individuals and their allies

Transfigured: a 40-day journey through scripture for gender-queer and transgender people

I Don't Want Them to Go to Hell: 50 days of encouragement for friends and families of LGBTQ people

Children's Books

Rumplepimple

Rumplepimple Goes to Jail

Pro-Life, Pro-Choice, Pro-Love

44 days of reflection for finding a third way in the abortion debate

Suzanne DeWitt Hall

Copyright © 2019 by Suzanne DeWitt Hall

All rights reserved. No part of this publication may be reproduced, distributed, or transmitted in any form or by any means, including photocopying, recording, or other electronic or mechanical methods, without the prior written permission of the publisher, except in the case of brief quotations embodied in critical reviews and certain other noncommercial uses permitted by copyright law.

DH Strategies

First Edition

ISBN-13: 978-0-9864080-7-6
ISBN-10: 0-9864080-7-7

Printed in the United States of America

Dedication

Abortion is an issue about motherhood and autonomy, and so I thought about the women who have provided various kinds of nurturing which we associate with mothering.

I thought about Jean Doremus; a great lady of grace who broke glass ceilings with gentleness and humor. She saw promise in me before I had actual skills, and steered me into a career which continues to aid my work even though I'm no longer constrained by a corporate environment.

I thought about Carol Crossed; a pioneer in wall-smashing activism who had a similar style of relentless, gentle, creativity. She showed me how to look beyond the edges of what other people are doing and saying, and to push back against labels.

But when it comes to nurturers, my heart always ends up in the hands of my beloved wife, Diane. My Dolce, who takes such good care of me, loves me, and encourages me every single day. Because of this, all my books will always be for Dolce, and through Dolce.

Arm in arm, sweetheart.

Contents

What Does God Think? 1
What Abortion Is and Isn't...17
Why Women Get Abortions 27
Check Your Privilege 45
Dealing with the Aftermath 57
What about Regulation? 65
Our Calling 83
Conclusion 93

INTRODUCTION

Pro-life? Pro-choice? How about pro-love.

I've had two abortions. The first was while I was in high school, and the second was a year or two after I graduated. Those experiences made me pro-life, and my view of abortion used to be resolute and concrete. The issue was as black and white as a barcode. But in recent years the demarcation between dark and light has blurred. Part of the blurring came from a conversation my wife and I had with a hospital chaplain. Here's what he said:

A soul stood at the gates of heaven, describing their life and hoping to be let in. They explained how they'd spent week after week picketing in front of abortion clinics, hoping to save the lives of unborn children. Jesus replied to them "Well done, my good and faithful servant! Come in and share my joy." And in they went. Then along came another soul, who explained how they accompanied a broken-hearted, desperate young woman to an abortion clinic so she wouldn't have to go alone. Jesus replied to them "Well done, my good and faithful servant! Come in and share my joy." And in they went.

The parable rocked me.

While it aligned with the kind of deeply compassionate evaluation I believe God applies to us, my adamant pro-life stance made it hard to know how to process what I heard. That conversation, coupled with the politics which have been unfolding over the past few years, prompted this book.

No matter how loudly either side screams about abortion being a black and white issue, it isn't. So let's be honest with ourselves, no matter which side of the hill you are willing to die on. Let's be honest with each other, which requires listening and processing before responding. Let's be honest about the complexity which saturates the issue of life's origins and women's autonomy.

Here are the questions I'd like you to consider as you work your way through this devotional:

- Can we reach a stage where we have mercy on the women who don't think they can or should give birth?
- Can we have mercy at the same time for the growing child in her womb?
- Can we have mercy on the healthcare professionals who believe with all sincerity that they are doing good in the world by providing abortion services?
- Can we attain the goal of viewing each of these groups through the eyes of Christ, our loving mediator and judge, who weighs our hearts and minds before rendering a judgment?

I wrote this book to try to figure out what I thought about the issue of abortion. I don't have many answers, but I do know that we should try to say *yes* to each of these questions.

#YouKnowMe References

During recent abortion rights rollbacks across the nation, a hashtag emerged for women to use when sharing stories about why they terminated pregnancies. #YouKnowMe appeared across social media, attached to descriptions of experiences which were hard to read. I've included a number of these stories from Twitter (without user names) to help move the debate away from the theoretical and into the personal. Because these were actual tweets, I've included them just as they are, with all the abbreviations and typos you'd expect in social media posts. Through them you'll encounter a lot of very real pain.

   I pray God uses that pain to enlighten all our hearts.

Guide to Translations

Abortion concerns people across all denominations. This devotional therefore includes a variety of Bible translations to reflect that diversity. Acronyms for included versions are listed below.

CEV	Contemporary English Version
ESV	English Standard Version
ISV	International Standard Version
KJV	King James Version
NAB	New American Bible
NABRE	New American Bible Revised Edition
NASB	New American Standard Bible
NIV	New International Version
NKJV	New King James Version
NRSV	New Revised Standard Version
NRSVCE	New Revised Standard Version Catholic Edition
RSV	Revised Standard Version

WHAT DOES GOD THINK?

As Christians we should all want to seek God's guidance about issues both important and small. Abortion is important. We're therefore starting our reflections by contemplating what God thinks, to set the stage for the remainder of the book.

The thoughts you'll encounter may seem conflicting.

That's because they are.

A Note about Pronouns

We are made in the male and female likeness of our Trinitarian God, who is three persons in one divine being. Because of this, you'll see that I refer to God as "they." If this is controversial to you, strap in. There's plenty more controversy to come.

Day 1: The Spirit Says "Listen!"

When the day of Pentecost had come, they were all together in one place. And suddenly from heaven there came a sound like the rush of a violent wind, and it filled the entire house where they were sitting. Divided tongues, as of fire, appeared among them, and a tongue rested on each of them. All of them were filled with the Holy Spirit and began to speak in other languages, as the Spirit gave them ability.

Now there were devout Jews from every nation under heaven living in Jerusalem. And at this sound the crowd gathered and was bewildered, because each one heard them speaking in the native language of each. Amazed and astonished, they asked, "Are not all these who are speaking Galileans? And how is it that we hear, each of us, in our own native language? Parthians, Medes, Elamites, and residents of Mesopotamia, Judea and Cappadocia, Pontus and Asia, Phrygia and Pamphylia, Egypt and the parts of Libya belonging to Cyrene, and visitors from Rome, both Jews and proselytes, Cretans and Arabs—in our own languages we hear them speaking about God's deeds of power." All were amazed and perplexed, saying to one another, "What does this mean?" But others sneered and said, "They are filled with new wine."
(Acts 2:1-13 NRSV)

Isn't the Pentecost story exciting, with its violent wind, tongues of fire, and sudden abilities to speak unknown languages? The scene is cinematic, and signaled a shift in the way the good news would be conveyed. Given all the astonishing sights and sounds, people had no choice but try to listen differently.

The abortion debate is one in which both sides have a great deal of trouble listening. We close our minds and hearts to what the other side is trying to say, neglecting the truths which are present in their messages. The heart of the Acts story is that through God, the lack of listening can and should be halted, and barriers to comprehension should be burnt away.

When the Spirit falls, amazing things happen. People who would not otherwise be able to hear a message can suddenly listen. People who normally don't convey information meaningfully are suddenly eloquent and persuasive.

Ask for the Spirit to fall upon you when reading this book. Put the Spirit in charge for opening your ears to hear the truth they want to whisper. And open your heart and mind to the ways in which you might need to alter your thinking.

Once you've done that, ask that you be able to speak the language of others. Transform what you've learned into verbal bridges to overcome barriers, so you can work toward real solutions for women in crisis pregnancy situations.

Isn't that what the good news is really about?

Life is not about "or" — it is about "and."
It is magical and messy.
It is heartwarming and heartbreaking.
It is delight and disappointment. Grace and grief.
Exquisite and excruciating, often at the exact same time.
Kristi Nelson

Day 2: God's Judgment

But with me it is a very small thing that I should be judged by you or by a human court. In fact, I do not even judge myself. For I know of nothing against myself, yet I am not justified by this; but He who judges me is the Lord. Therefore judge nothing before the time, until the Lord comes, who will both bring to light the hidden things of darkness and reveal the counsels of the hearts.
(1 Corinthians 4:3-5 NKJV)

The entire premise of this devotional is built around a particular understanding of God. Here's the theology in a nutshell:

1. Jesus came to correct our faulty understanding of the divine, and to show us that God is love. (1 John 4:7-8)
2. Jesus is our judge (John 5:2), full of compassion (James 5:11) and was tempted like us in all ways (Hebrews 4:15) which means he can judge us with empathy because he understands our stressors and emotions.
3. The final judgment is based on how well we extend compassion and mercy to others. We are judged sheep or goats based on those actions. (Matthew 25:31-46)

This approach to judgment applies to everything: the little white lies we tell, the superiority we feel toward our neighbors, the lusting and infidelity we indulge in, and every other ungodly act we commit with our minds, hearts, or bodies.

Judgment is not binary. It's not an on/off switch of right versus wrong. It's an evaluation of evidence, and in the case of God's judgment our Creator, Redeemer, and Advocate walks through our actions with us, knowing what drove us, knowing what pain and brokenness we experience, knowing all the whys we ourselves don't even understand.

Those who get abortions, those who counsel for abortion, and those who perform abortions are all judged the same way. They are all subject to the same intimacy of judgment. The same loving, compassionate, empathetic understanding.

If you can't embrace this theology, the book in your hands right now isn't for you. You might as well put it down and remain right where you are.

If you are able to embrace the good news this understanding of God delivers, read on.

> *He is a Christian who shows compassion to all, who is not at all provoked by wrong done to him, who does not allow the poor to be oppressed in his presence, who helps the wretched, who succors the needy, who mourns with the mourners, who feels another's pain as if it were his own, who is moved to tears by the tears of others…*
> Pelagius

Day 3: God's Abortion Juice

Then the Lord said to Moses, "Speak to the Israelites and say to them: 'If a man's wife goes astray and is unfaithful to him so that another man has sexual relations with her, and this is hidden from her husband and her impurity is undetected (since there is no witness against her and she has not been caught in the act), and if feelings of jealousy come over her husband and he suspects his wife and she is impure—or if he is jealous and suspects her even though she is not impure— then he is to take his wife to the priest. He must also take an offering of a tenth of an ephah of barley flour on her behalf. He must not pour olive oil on it or put incense on it, because it is a grain offering for jealousy, a reminder-offering to draw attention to wrongdoing. The priest shall bring her and have her stand before the Lord. Then he shall take some holy water in a clay jar and put some dust from the tabernacle floor into the water. After the priest has had the woman stand before the Lord, he shall loosen her hair and place in her hands the reminder-offering, the grain offering for jealousy, while he himself holds the bitter water that brings a curse. Then the priest shall put the woman under oath and say to her, "If no other man has had sexual relations with you and you have not gone astray and become impure while married to your husband, may this bitter water that brings a curse not harm you. But if you have gone astray while married to your husband and you have made yourself impure by having sexual relations with a man other than your husband"— here the priest is to put the woman under this curse—"may the Lord cause you to become a curse among your people when he makes your womb miscarry and your abdomen swell. May this water that brings a curse enter your body so that your abdomen swells or your womb miscarries."
(Numbers 5:11-22 NIV)

Some Christians hold the scriptures in such esteem that they might as well be added as a fourth person to the Trinity. They use Bible passages selectively to defend their positions on all sorts of issues, while ignoring countless others which might contraindicate their points.

Today's verses are one example, and they're hard for pro-life Christians to think about. They should be hard for *any* Christian to consider, because our God of love doesn't seem to be reflected in them.

Women accused of adultery were shamed and forced to drink the bitter dirt-water whether they were guilty or not. And if they *were* guilty, according to the very words of God in this passage, any children which had been conceived would be aborted.

Intentionally.

At God's order.

There is only one direct reference to abortion in the Bible, and this is it; God's recipe for brewing abortion juice.

One of my goals in starting this devotional with a section on how the Bible portrays God's view is to point out that it's complicated.

So what are we to make of this?

If the unborn is not a human person, no justification for abortion is necessary. However, if the unborn is a human person, no justification for abortion is adequate.
Greg Kouki

Day 4: God Knows Us in the Womb

Before I formed you in the womb I knew you, and before you were born I consecrated you; I appointed you a prophet to the nations.
(Jeremiah 1:5 ESV)

The divine is present in all things, but Christians tend to view humans as more fully manifesting that presence due to our intellect, our creativity, and the dominance our opposable thumbs provide. We look at scripture and see that we are made in the image and likeness of God, which confirms our presumed superiority. But if we were able to look closely enough into the being of a dog or cat in a rescue shelter, or a leaf of grass on the side of a highway, or the pseudopod of an amoeba in our favorite lake, we would surely be able to recognize the divinity residing there, in all its shining purity.

Today we read about God speaking to Jeremiah, assuring him of his role as prophet and the preparation which was underway for that role from the days when he was merely a collection of rapidly reproducing cells.

Humans are unrepeatable. The uniqueness begins the moment a sperm cell penetrates the wall of an egg, and the miraculous mixing of two becomes one. The being that is the particular combination of a particular sperm and a particular egg cannot ever be recreated.

Of course there are many things which can go wrong in the course of fetal development, causing an embryo to be miscarried, often without a woman realizing she was ever pregnant in the first place. But that doesn't change the fact that the tiny potential being implanted within her was entirely unique, and entirely imbued with the presence of God.

Before God forms us in the womb they know us.

We can't have reasoned discussion about abortion without acknowledging this Christian understanding of the divinity within all creation.

We can't pretend fetuses aren't tiny people.

> *I know this issue is very controversial. But unless and until it can be proven that an unborn child is not a human being, can we justify assuming without proof that it isn't? No one has yet offered such proof; indeed, all the evidence is to the contrary. We should rise above bitterness and reproach, and if Americans could come together in a spirit of understanding and helping, then we could find positive solutions to the tragedy of abortion.*
> Ronald Reagan

Day 5: Souls are Infinite

Since we have the same spirit of faith as he had who wrote, "I believed, and so I spoke," we too believe, and so we speak, knowing that he who raised the Lord Jesus will raise us also with Jesus and bring us with you into his presence. For it is all for your sake, so that as grace extends to more and more people it may increase thanksgiving, to the glory of God.

So we do not lose heart. Though our outer nature is wasting away, our inner nature is being renewed every day. For this slight momentary affliction is preparing for us an eternal weight of glory beyond all comparison, because we look not to the things that are seen but to the things that are unseen; for the things that are seen are transient, but the things that are unseen are eternal.
(2 Corinthians 4:13-18 RSVCE)

We don't really know why God creates souls. The Baltimore and Westminster Catechisms tell us we come into being to love and worship God, and to be happy with God forever in heaven. But this still doesn't explain *why*.

We also don't know when souls are fused with bodies to become unique humans. We don't know if it's the microsecond in which the sperm penetrates the egg, or if it's at the first division of cells, or at some other point along the chain of human development.

Neither do we know what happens to us when our bodies die. We get a few glimpses of the afterlife in the scriptures, with streets of gold and perpetually singing angels. Near-death experience reports differ significantly from biblical visions however, and are typically much less corporeal, and much more mystical. They are less a contiguous representation of bodily existence in some sort of resurrected form, and more focused on union and ecstatic experience of energy and light.

This combination of unknowns makes me wonder: is it really necessary for humans to be born in order to fulfill God's design? Let's say the soul is in place very early, even immediately at the explosive union of sperm and egg. Could not this new creation, unstained and untouched by the selfishness and hatred which so frequently characterizes our species, become joyously part of the heavenly throng of singing stars and molecules just as the freed soul of a desperately ill octogenarian does?

Make no mistake; I view life as sacred; all life, from the earliest moments to the final. But I also think that sacredness far transcends what our limited intellects can conceive. It is far more vast than the constraints of being born and sent off to kindergarten, of partnering and parenting, of learning and teaching, of loving and eventually dying.

Perhaps these tiny unborn souls are more purely ready to greet and be greeted by God than I am, sitting her writing to you and judging my neighbor. More than the politicians and clergy who preach gospels of blame and exclusion. Perhaps these little unpolluted souls have much to teach us, and will greet us when we become as untethered to the merely physical as they are.

One day you will see that what must be born will be born. Everything else will find another way.
Naomi Jackson

Day 6: God's Murder of Babies

*Daughter Babylon, doomed to destruction,
happy is the one who repays you
according to what you have done to us.
Happy is the one who seizes your infants
and dashes them against the rocks.*
(Psalm 137:7-9 NIV)

Many opponents of abortion view it as objectionable for religious reasons. But we are faced with a dilemma when it comes to biblical treatment of infants, particularly in the Hebrew Scriptures. There are numerous stories of God initiating the death of babies, starting right in Exodus when the Egyptians refused to let the Israelites go. Deuteronomy 28 includes a list of curses from God for disobedience which include a number of gruesome passages about mothers and fathers eating the flesh of their children, and not sharing it with their other offspring. Isaiah 13 gives us descriptions of God's wrath on Babylon, with infants being dashed to pieces, and babies being put to death in the womb. In Hosea 9 we see promises to disobedient Ephraim to put their children to death and give them miscarrying wombs. Hosea 13 tells us that the winds of the Lord would come and that pregnant women would be ripped open. Then there are the accounts of the wanderer's conquest of the promised land in Joshua 6, when God ordered the destruction of all life, including babies both in and out of the womb.

Given the numerous texts describing God's desire to kill babies both before and after their births, it *should* be hard to justify a biblical stance for protecting the unborn for those who lean toward a view of scripture as inspired, inerrant, and infallible. According to the Bible, killing babies was the just, right, and proper thing to do for a variety of reasons and by a variety of methods.

It seems fair to say that most Christians are troubled by these passages. They are unsettling and many are grotesque. We can agree that they don't line up with the truth of God as love which we see revealed through Jesus Christ.

Most of us understand the wonder of babies in formation, with all they promise. And that's what creates the problem. Pro-life people are good at acknowledging the wonder, and bad at acknowledging the complexity of development and the mother's situation. Pro-choice people are good at acknowledging the difficulty of life here on earth, but dismiss the wonder and relegate nascent life to phrases like "clump of cells," calling the child "a pregnancy" or simply "the fetus" to try to remove the humanity.

The Hebrew scriptures show us a view which acknowledges that the fruit of the womb are children, and the heartbreak women face when they lose them, but it also offers fairly frequent examples of the murder of babies being the will of God.

I ask again, then: what are we to make of all this?

What might be a third way?

Over the centuries, and even today, the Bible and Christian theology have helped justify the Crusades, slavery, violence against gays, and the murder of doctors who perform abortions. The words themselves are latent, inert, harmless—until they aren't.
Amy Waldman

WHAT DOES GOD THINK?

DAY 7: GOD PERMITS CHOICE

In the sixth month the angel Gabriel was sent from God to a city of Galilee named Nazareth, to a virgin betrothed to a man whose name was Joseph, of the house of David. And the virgin's name was Mary. And he came to her and said, "Greetings, O favored one, the Lord is with you!" But she was greatly troubled at the saying, and tried to discern what sort of greeting this might be. And the angel said to her, "Do not be afraid, Mary, for you have found favor with God. And behold, you will conceive in your womb and bear a son, and you shall call his name Jesus. He will be great and will be called the Son of the Most High. And the Lord God will give to him the throne of his father David, and he will reign over the house of Jacob forever, and of his kingdom there will be no end."

And Mary said to the angel, "How will this be, since I am a virgin?"

And the angel answered her, "The Holy Spirit will come upon you, and the power of the Most High will overshadow you; therefore the child to be born will be called holy—the Son of God. And behold, your relative Elizabeth in her old age has also conceived a son, and this is the sixth month with her who was called barren. For nothing will be impossible with God." And Mary said, "Behold, I am the servant of the Lord; let it be to me according to your word." And the angel departed from her.
(Luke 1:26-38 ESV)

The story of Jesus's conception is a gorgeous unfolding of what took place when the Holy Spirit fell upon Mary and impregnated her. From the earliest days of the church, Christians have pondered Mary's fiat; her "yes," to God's request.

The fact that she gave her assent shows us that God would also have respected her "no."

Consider this woman's #YouKnowMe story of approaching an abortion clinic:

It was my first week of college when I found out I was pregnant with my abusive ex's baby. It wasn't an easy decision, protestors threw bags of pigs blood at me, and I still think about it daily. But I know I did what was best for me and I'm not ashamed.

The young woman's experience haunts her to this day. When I read her account, I thought about what Mary's reality must have been like as an unwed mother, and what she would have done if people had tried to talk her out of her decision, or tried to stone her as she went about town, or threw pig's blood or excrement at her.

In his final words on the cross, Jesus gave Mary to be mother of us all. She is our mother now: yours and mine, the protestor at an abortion clinic, and the desperate college student hurrying inside with hunched shoulders and a broken heart. Mother to Jesus, and mother to all of us. A model of the power to choose.

From the very beginning, God offered us choice. God respects our ability to choose, and has made it a central element of our existence.

If God found it important to ask a woman whether or not she wanted to carry a child, SO SHOULD EVERYONE ELSE. If God allows time for the conversation, the questioning, the pushback, SO SHOULD EVERYONE ELSE. It matters. It matters! It matters to me. And the more time I've spent reading and learning about scripture, Mary, my God and myself? The more deeply I'm convinced this matters to God, too. Women must be afforded the ability to consent *to carry pregnancies. Mary was given that opportunity.*
Hannah Shanks

DAY 8: GOOD ADVICE IS OFTEN WRONG

After the Lord had said these things to Job, he said to Eliphaz the Temanite, "I am angry with you and your two friends, because you have not spoken the truth about me, as my servant Job has. So now take seven bulls and seven rams and go to my servant Job and sacrifice a burnt offering for yourselves. My servant Job will pray for you, and I will accept his prayer and not deal with you according to your folly. You have not spoken the truth about me, as my servant Job has."
(Job 42:7-9 NIV)

Job's friends offered what sounded like good advice; he must have been screwing up or God wouldn't be punishing him the way they were. It was based on a common understanding of who God was, which persists down until today. We are quick to offer opinions and advice to people who are in all kinds of emotional and other trouble. Quick to tell a desperate pregnant girl to abort the baby or to keep it, quick to say why, quick to point out the need for freedom or the potential for damnation. We are quick to assume we know the heart of God and eager to state it with great authority. But "good advice" is often wrong.

Perhaps instead of simply passing along a canned response based on your entrenched views of abortion, you can listen prayerfully for the voice of Christ before speaking. Perhaps you can take a moment to realize that we don't actually have a black and white god, but a God of compassion, mercy, and understanding. And after taking that time, perhaps the advice you offer can be a purer reflection of divine love for the soul they are entrusting to you in that moment.

When an individual woman faces the decision whether to terminate a pregnancy, the issue is intensely personal, and may manifest itself in ways that do not reflect public rhetoric, or do not fit neatly into medical, legal or policy guidelines. Humans are empowered by the spirit prayerfully to make significant moral choices, including the choice to continue or end a pregnancy. Human choices should not be made in a moral vacuum, but must be based on Scripture, faith and Christian ethics. For any choice, we are accountable to God; however, even when we err, God offers to forgive us.
217th General Assembly (2006), Presbyterian Church (U.S.A.)

WHAT ABORTION IS AND ISN'T

In this section we'll cover a few topics which might make you uncomfortable if you consider yourself pro-choice. Try to stick with it. Remember: this book views abortion from both sides.

DAY 9: ABORTION IS THE UN-CHOICE

"For I know the plans I have for you," declares the Lord, "plans to prosper you and not to harm you, plans to give you hope and a future.
(Jeremiah 29:11 NIB)

A decade ago I worked in various aspects of the pro-life movement. For a few years I researched and raised awareness about the risks and side-effects of abortion for an organization that no longer exists. In another job, I studied the demographics of people who sought abortion services, including surveys of why women thought they needed them. What I concluded is that for most women, abortion is the very opposite of choice. It's the thing you do because you feel you have *no other* choice. It's an act of desperation for someone who feels trapped.

The latest data reported by the Guttmacher Institute (a research organization affiliated with Planned Parenthood) is from 2014. According to that data[1], 23.2% of abortion patients were teenagers. Another 34% were aged 20-24. Many of the young adults were college students. Most were poor.

What this tells us is that the majority of women who get abortions are essentially kids. They feel trapped by circumstances of finance, family, or romantic relationship. They feel like they have *no choice* but abort. They long for the future and the hope today's scripture passage promises, but they simply can't see it.

"A woman's right to choose" is the rallying cry of the pro-choice movement, and I get the concept of a woman choosing whether to continue a pregnancy or terminate it. It does require a decision, and decisions involve making choices, but are the grasping choices we're forced to make during desperate times to ensure our survival real choices? When a mother steals food to feed starving children, is she actually *choosing* to commit a crime? When a teenager is kicked out of their house because of an LGBTQ+ identity and targeted by a

---

[1] Induced Abortion in the United States, Guttmacher Institute, September 2019

human trafficker, are they really *choosing* to be a sex worker? When a victim of repeated domestic violence doesn't report the last time her partner beats her because she's afraid he'll kill her, is she truly *choosing* to be abused?

Are any of these things real choices?

Many women who have abortions don't feel this degree of desperation, and are able to rationally determine whether to continue a pregnancy based on the various aspects of their lives which contribute to the decision. But many—I'd submit *most*—*do* experience the kind of duress which significantly compromises decision making.

Because of this, abortion is really the un-choice. It's the thing we do when we believe there is no other choice.

How does this reality impact our view of the debate?

How should it inform our decision making?

What does it contribute to our prayer and action?

It surprises me, though it shouldn't, how short the memories of these politicians are. They forget the brutal lengths women have gone to in order to terminate pregnancies when abortion was illegal or when abortion is unaffordable. Women have thrown themselves down stairs and otherwise tried to physically harm themselves to force a miscarriage. Dr. Waldo Fielding noted in the New York Times, "Almost any implement you can imagine had been and was used to start an abortion—darning needles, crochet hooks, cut-glass salt shakers, soda bottles, sometimes intact, sometimes with the top broken off." Women have tried to use soap and bleach, catheters, natural remedies. Women have historically resorted to any means necessary. Women will do this again if we are backed into that terrible corner. This is the responsibility our society has forced on women for hundreds of years.
Roxane Gay

WHAT ABORTION IS AND ISN'T

Day 10: Abortion Is the Death of a Baby

For behold, when the sound of your greeting came to my ears, the baby in my womb leaped for joy.
(Luke 1:44 ESV)

I once met a young woman who didn't realize that abortion ended the life of a baby. She was a naïve soul, but when she discovered what was actually happening, she was shocked.

Terminology matters.

The pro-choice movement has worked hard to make sure phrases related to what's growing in the wombs of women don't imply nascent humanity. The tiny creature is referred to as a "clump of cells" to reduce it to something merely observable on the slide of a microscope, or "the pregnancy" to connote a medical condition, or "a fetus" because biological terms aren't something which typically have emotional hooks.

It makes sense that proponents would do this from a marketing perspective. Let's face it; talking about scraping a baby from a woman's womb is harsh. We don't respond well to the tangible facts of what happens during abortion. When we stop to consider what is happening physically to the forming child, it's jarring, and we respond emotionally.

Which we should do.

But abortion advocates should be willing to say what is actually happening. Honesty is important. Yes, the fetus is "merely" potential life, but there's no demarcation in the transition from potential to actual for when one state becomes the other. The heartbeat begins remarkably early—at about five weeks—and subsequent changes continue at a rapid pace, transforming from the potential that was two cells into what is pretty quickly a child who could survive outside the womb with the right kind of medical care.

The thing growing inside a woman's uterus is a baby. Pretending this isn't the case does the discussion a disservice. It does the women considering the procedure a disservice, and leads to a lack of true consent.

I'm sorry if it bothers you to face this reality, but it has to be faced. Scripture tells us to "let our yes be yes," and that applies to a whole lot more than merely avoiding making oaths. It also means that we need to know what we are actually saying yes to.

> *Abortion is inherently different from other medical procedures because no other procedure involves the purposeful termination of a potential life.*
> Potter Stewart

Day 11: Abortion Isn't Between a Woman and Her Doctor

*The Lord is near to the brokenhearted,
and saves the crushed in spirit.*
(Psalm 34:18 RSV)

In debates about the abortion issue, you often hear phrases like "the decision should be between a woman and her doctor." It sounds so logical and safe, doesn't it? After all, who else do we trust to help us make medical decisions? The ones who are familiar with our medical histories, and know the interconnections which might make various procedures or medications problematic. But this is rarely the case. Millions of women (particularly young women) never go to their doctors in crisis pregnancy situations. They go to a clinic, hoping for anonymity (because God help them if their family finds out), or because it's cheap, or because they don't have an OB/GYN.

When they arrive for the procedure, there may or may not be a medical doctor present. The Planned Parenthood website offers descriptions of several abortion procedures stating that a doctor *or* a nurse will perform them.[2] Some states require that a doctor with admitting privileges at a local hospital be on staff, in case things go wrong, which they sometimes (though rarely) do. Abortion advocate organizations consider this an onerous burden.

Some women *do* go to their OB/GYN when in crisis pregnancy, and *do* talk it through with a physician who knows their health history. But many—probably most—do not. Many—probably most—abort in clinic settings where their history is completely unknown, and where follow up care is unlikely to take place.

While they are making up their minds they aren't talking to a doctor. They are talking to some sort of admissions person, and potentially a nurse. They typically won't see a doctor until they are in the procedure room, and they might not see an actual doctor even then.

---

[2] What Happens During an In-Clinic Abortion? Planned Parenthood Federation of America, Inc. website

Women show up at these places crushed and brokenhearted, as today's scripture describes. Many abortions are hidden. They often aren't a real choice, and they are not typically made between a woman and her doctor.

So let's stop using that phrase, and let's start doing a better job of serving the girls and women who end up receiving completely anonymous services in these clinics.

Informed consent has gained increasing salience within the health care field. The need to secure a patient's fully-informed consent prior to medical intervention for treatment or research purposes is increasingly heralded as an ethical panacea counteracting the potential danger of paternalistic and autocratic practices.
Oonagh Corrigan

What Abortion Is and Isn't

Day 12: Abortion Is Sometimes Healthcare

> *'For I will restore health to you*
> *And heal you of your wounds,' says the Lord,*
> *'Because they called you an outcast saying:*
> *"This is Zion;*
> *No one seeks her."'*
> (Jeremiah 30:17 NKJV)

For many years I was affronted when I heard the term "healthcare" used to describe abortion. It seemed wildly inappropriate given that pregnancy is not illness or disorder. It's a natural, healthy state in most cases. Because of this, it seemed like logic manipulation to refer to abortion procedures as "healthcare services."

But when I checked the definition recently, I saw something I'd overlooked: healthcare refers to both physical *and* mental health. This means there's an argument to be made that in some cases, abortion can in fact be a treatment option for managing emotional unwellness. There are also a number of pregnancy-induced health crises which render abortion as care for the mother. We'll read about some of these issues in the next section.

I feel conflicted about all this. Some of the #YouKnowMe tweets are casual and nearly callous, claiming their abortions were no big deal and (essentially) an easy fix to an annoying problem. I can't view abortion as healthcare in that kind of situation, though these people *could* be sublimating the impact, as many of us do.

Yes, surgical abortion always involves medical procedures, but is it curative? Is it preventive?

In cases like this, are we supposed to believe it's like an emotional teeth cleaning, in which mental health is theoretically protected by pre-removing a potential stressor?

I feel conflicted about this. And I hope you do too.

Seeing modern health care from the other side, I can say that it is clearly not set up for the patient. It is frequently a poor arrangement for doctors as well, but that does not mitigate how little the system accounts for the patient's best interest. Just when you are at your weakest and least able to make all the phone calls, traverse the maze of insurance, and plead for health-care referrals is that one time when you have to your life may depend on it.
Ross Donaldson

What Abortion Is and Isn't

Why Women Get Abortions

In this section we'll ponder some of the reasons women choose to end their pregnancies. These contemplations are designed to help us develop compassion for the varied circumstances which drive people to the decision.

Day 13: Desperation

I am desperate
Because God All-Powerful
refuses
to do what is right.
(Job 27:2 CEV)

When I searched for Bible passages about desperation, the words of Job came up, including today's verses which have been translated in a particularly poignant way.

Women seeking abortions are desperate. The experience of watching and waiting for your period to arrive is nearly universal for heterosexually active women who had slip-ups with birth control (or worse.) The worry consumes you; fear that you might be pregnant surges in and out of the day. Prayers rise from scared teenagers who promise God if they aren't pregnant then next time they'll be more careful, or insist he use a condom, or even stop having sex altogether. Prayers rise from devastatingly poor mothers who can't afford to feed their existing children, and don't know how they'll fill another mouth. Prayers rise from partners of physically abusive men, who've made it clear things will be very, very bad if they get pregnant. Prayers ascend from all these people, beseeching God for help.

The prayers change when their periods don't arrive and their breasts grow tender; when they pee on a stick or in a cup and find out their worst fears have been confirmed. The prayer changes to the words of Job:

God all-powerful refuses to do what is right.

At that moment, it feels like God refuses to do what is right for their emotional stability, for their family or relationship structure, or for their present and future economic stability.

Here are two #YouKnowMe stories from women in this kind of extremis:

I was in an abusive relationship & had 2 kids by him. I had already lost one baby by him due to his assaults. After that I was on bc & got pregnant. I had an abortion very early on bc I knew I would never escape. Took 4 more years for us to get out.

I was 23, broke, suffering with clinical depression, in physical pain, and terrified. My thought was suicide or #abortion...I chose wisely.

Desperation is a horrible thing. The scriptures are filled with stories of desperate people begging for help. The Creator obviously desires wholeness and pleasure for us, because promises of abundance and satisfaction fill page after page, and glorious visions of these things are presented as the conclusion of our faith lives. God wasn't pleased by Job's friends leaving him alone in his desperate moments. We shouldn't leave these desperate women alone in their times of distress, either. If we demand that abortion should be illegal and work toward that end, we must also work toward helping the frightened girls and women who can no longer see a way out.

Fighting to change abortion laws and picketing clinics is easy. It's removed from the very real humanity whose desperation is tangible and whose pain elicits Jesus' tears. God is not pleased that their anguish is ignored.

I urge you; for every email, text, or phone call to a legislator in favor of restricting abortion access, and every hour you spend on social media or outside abortion clinics, devote the same amount of time and energy into finding actual solutions for these women.

God cares about the individual. Every hair on every head is numbered. God is not pleased that these beloved wounded are sacrificed and ignored on the altar of a movement.

A significant driver of opposition to abortion is the social construction of the Ideal Woman. In a culture that rarely, if ever, allows women simply to be people, value is ascribed based on a woman's relation to something other than herself. A woman on her own is like a bit of driftwood floating in the ocean. She is a broken object with no purpose, waiting either to wash up on the shore and be put to use as part of something else, or to sink and be forgotten forever.
Clementine Ford

Day 14: Failed Contraception

Come now, you who say, "Today or tomorrow we will go into such and such a town and spend a year there and trade and make a profit"—yet you do not know what tomorrow will bring. What is your life? For you are a mist that appears for a little time and then vanishes. Instead you ought to say, "If the Lord wills, we will live and do this or that." As it is, you boast in your arrogance. All such boasting is evil.
(James 4:13-16 ESV)

"Mann tracht, un Gott lacht" is an old Yiddish adage which means essentially that humans plan and God laughs.

Have you ever developed a really great plan that fell apart? Maybe it was for a dream vacation or a home renovation. Maybe it was a career plan or a project at work. Maybe it was for a relationship or even a marriage. The things we line up to ensure a desired outcome frequently fail, despite our diligence.

While researching this book I came across a sorrowful number of pro-life voices bombasting that unplanned pregnancy is the result of irresponsibility or laziness. But in reading #YouKnowMe stories, I discovered that failed contraception is a common phenomenon. Here are four examples of this situation:

I was 15. I was studying for my GCSEs. Birth control failed me. My boyfriend threatened to throw me down the stairs because he didn't want his parents to know. It changed my path. It changed my life. Women deserve the right of choice.

At 19 years old, I had an abortion. I was walking my child through kidney failure. I didn't have the time or energy to split my attention between my gravely ill child and a new baby, but my birth control failed. If I hadn't had access to an abortion at that time in my life, one of my children would have been completely neglected out of necessity of caring for the other.

We had a toddler and 6 month old. In treatment for severe postpartum depression and contraceptives failed. Zero regrets.

> *I'm an MD, adoptive mother of 3. I aborted a pregnancy w/ a deadend boyfriend when birth control failed (diaphragm and condom simultaneously) 2 months before starting medical school. I've done more good as an MD Then I would have as a single, poverty-stricken parent.*

In each of these scenarios, birth control was used. The women were responsible sexually. But no method is 100% effective. Our plans and actions to control conception while sexually active are just as prone to failure as all our other plans for shaping our futures.

Today's James passage shows us that boasting about our ability to control outcomes is arrogance. The author goes so far as to call it evil. Judging women when their plans for conception fail is even worse.

> *I want a future abortion conversation known for its openness, respect, and empathy, so instead of generating more heat, anger, and conflict, I practice pro-voice.*
> Aspen Baker

Day 15: Health of the Mother

The human spirit can endure in sickness,
but a crushed spirit who can bear?
(Proverbs 18:14 NIV)

When my views were purely pro-life, I believed there were no situations in which abortion would save the life of the mother.

I was wrong.

The majority of people who have abortions report reasons related to finances, relationships, or the ability to care for a child. Very few report their reasons as concerns about their own health, but those cases are real. Some health problems cited include cancer, cystic fibrosis, and other chronic and debilitating conditions.[3]

Pregnancy-related problems can also create crisis situations. A 44-year-old writer from Pennsylvania developed severe preeclampsia when she was six months pregnant with twins in 2004. One of the babies died, and the mother's liver and kidneys had shut down. An abortion on the remaining baby was performed in order to save the woman's life. Her spirit was crushed from having to make the decision to abort. She was terribly ill, but the last thing she wanted was to have to end her pregnancy. She and her husband wanted the babies, and losing them was heartbreaking. Since this happened she's written about it to help process her grief. "I fought it," she says. "But they told me I would die; that it was either me and my son or just my son."[4]

Here's a #YouKnowMe report of another life-and-death situation:

The baby was not viable, and I had to have an abortion before starting chemo.
It was devastating. And necessary. It broke my heart. And it was a decision
best left between myself and my health care provider.

---

[3] Reasons U.S. Women Have Abortions: Quantitative and Qualitative Perspectives, by Lawrence B. Finer et al., US National Library of Medicine National Institutes of Health, September 2005

[4] Doctors Say Abortions do Sometimes Save Women's Lives, USA Today, October 2012

People who face this kind of a crossroad endure a unique heartache. Condemnation for making a choice which felt like no choice only heaps stones on what is an already spirit-crushing weight.

If you're convinced (as I was) that there are no health situations which require abortion to save the life of a mother, please do more research. The stories are real, and powerful, and painful.

Your religion should help you make the decision if you find yourself in that situation, but the policy should exist for you to have the right to make it in the first place. When you say you can't do something because your religion forbids it, that's a good thing. When you say I can't do something because YOUR religion forbids it, that's a problem.
Jodi Picoult

Day 16: Ectopic Pregnancy

Jesus said: "A man was going down from Jerusalem to Jericho, when he was attacked by robbers. They stripped him of his clothes, beat him and went away, leaving him half dead. A priest happened to be going down the same road, and when he saw the man, he passed by on the other side. So too, a Levite, when he came to the place and saw him, passed by on the other side. But a Samaritan, as he traveled, came where the man was; and when he saw him, he took pity on him. He went to him and bandaged his wounds, pouring on oil and wine. Then he put the man on his own donkey, brought him to an inn and took care of him. The next day he took out two denarii and gave them to the innkeeper. 'Look after him,' he said, 'and when I return, I will reimburse you for any extra expense you may have.'
"Which of these three do you think was a neighbor to the man who fell into the hands of robbers?"
The expert in the law replied, "The one who had mercy on him."
Jesus told him, "Go and do likewise."
(Luke 10:30-37 NIV)

At the time of this book's writing, bills at the state level were being considered to make aborting ectopic pregnancies illegal. An ectopic pregnancy takes place when a fertilized egg attaches itself somewhere outside the uterus, where survival is not possible. In most cases, it happens in a fallopian tube, and without removal, the tube will burst causing internal bleeding and potentially, death.

Here's one woman's story from Twitter:

At 8 wks my life was in danger d/t an #ectopic pregnancy. My fallopian tube had ruptured & I was bleeding to death. But the embryo still had a "heartbeat". The doctor at the ER told me I was smart to have come to them bc if I had gone to the Catholic hospital in town. They would have made keep bleeding until the "heartbeat" stopped, and only then acted to save my life. I remember feeling an overwhelming anger on top of my overwhelming fear & grief, thinking about some poor woman sitting in their ER at that same moment, not having my same care.

When considering what this poor woman was dealing with, which of these hospitals could treat her in the way Jesus instructs through the Good Samaritan parable?

Regardless of how pro-life your stance, shouldn't procedures be safe and legal when they end the existence of an embryo which simply cannot survive, in order that the woman who carries it can live?

If we cannot love our neighbor as ourself, it is because we do not perceive our neighbor as ourself.
Beatrice Bruteau

Day 17: Health of the Baby

He will wipe away every tear from their eyes, and death shall be no more, neither shall there be mourning, nor crying, nor pain anymore, for the former things have passed away.
(Revelation 21:4 ESV)

As discussed previously, most abortions are sought because of a woman's inability to properly care for a child financially, emotionally, or relationtionally. But sometimes women who had every intention of getting pregnant, or were happily surprised, or were unhappily surprised but planned to carry the child to term, find out terrible news: there's a health problem with the child. The heartbreak of learning that the life you'd built dreams around won't come to fruition is devastating.

Here are a few heartbreaking stories of health crises in utero, from the #YouKnowMe threads:

It was 1975. I was a new mom. And had just found out that the medications my doctor prescribed to prevent suicide during my postpartum psychosis had a very high probability of producing a limbless child. What else could I do?

I had an abortion in 1991 because of multiple fetal abnormalities. The baby would have been born dead or had a short miserable life. My trusted Dr. wouldn't perform the procedure, I had to go somewhere else. That made a difficult situation harder.

I was 26, happily married and excited for the pregnancy. We got a non compatible with life diagnosis - the skull didn't form. We ended the pregnancy at 13 weeks. We made the best choice for us and now have a happy and healthy baby

I had a second trimester abortion. My baby hadn't formed his kidneys correctly and there wasn't enough amniotic fluid. His chance of making it to birth was slim, and of living past birth nonexistent. It was not a decision made lightly and I am not a criminal.

> *I was 19, strung out on heroin, living on the streets, malnourished, with no intentions of staying clean. I was told the baby was underdeveloped and most likely developmentally disabled. I made a hard decision that I don't regret.*

These examples offer a glimpse of the breadth of health problems a forming infant can experience, along with some of the reasons women choose not to continue their pregnancies.

In some Christian views, the mother is expected to carry the baby as long as possible, and let God unfold the child's life in whatever way their Creator deigns, which means giving birth and waiting for the child to die "naturally." Some women choose this option, finding ways to cope with the anguish of what is to come. Others simply can't manage.

The question for you today is, should they have to?

Does God demand this of them?

> *My argument has always been that nature has a master plan pushing every species toward procreation and that it is our right and even obligation as rational human beings to defy nature's fascism. Nature herself is a mass murderer, making casual, cruel experiments and condemning 10,000 to die so that one more fit will live and thrive.*
> Camille Paglia

Day 18: Rape

But if it is in the open fields that a man comes upon the betrothed young woman, seizes her and lies with her, only the man who lay with her shall die. You shall do nothing to the young woman, since the young woman is not guilty of a capital offense. As when a man rises up against his neighbor and murders him, so in this case: it was in the open fields that he came upon her, and though the betrothed young woman may have cried out, there was no one to save her.
(Deuteronomy 22:25-27 NABRE)

In the years I did pro-life work I came across a number of accounts about women who carried babies conceived through rape to term. Some raised the children and unfolded stories of the great grace in their lives which resulted. But of course, this isn't always the case. Here are a few #YouKnowMe stories about this topic.

I was raped as a teen. My Catholic adoptive mom said she wouldn't allow an abortion if I was pregnant. She wanted my rapist and I to marry. In between waiting and fighting to testify and a false positive, I planned my suicide.

I was 13 and got raped I ended up pregnant without knowing until I'd miscarried. If I hadn't, I would have needed an abortion bc the baby would have killed me.

I was gang raped at 17 and became pregnant with one of my 6 rapists baby. I decided to have an abortion which helped me heal from being traumatized. I'm 34 now and never once regretted my decision. As a mother now I'm terrified for my daughter

Rape carries with it a host of lifelong emotional and psychological baggage and damage. Rape is an action of violence and control, and the victim feels a profound loss of autonomy as a result. Having no choice but to carry the child conceived through that violence is a continuation of the raping of self-determination. It's a continuation of that aspect of the crime.

The child who is busily multiplying itself within the victim's body doesn't know or care how its life began. But does that innocence override the innocence stolen from the woman who was assaulted? Shouldn't she have the opportunity to make her own decision, when the ramifications are so profound, and when the situation arose from being raped of choice?

Is there enough compassion in God's heart for women to be able to exercise the autonomy which rapists stole from them?

> *You just raped every woman who's been raped by a man. You just raped her all over again. This is just a shame, this is a disgrace, this is a travesty.*
> Senate Minority Leader Bobby Singleton, D-Greensboro, Alabama

Day 19: Incest

> *One commits abomination with his neighbor's wife; another lewdly defiles his daughter-in-law; and another in you violates his sister, his father's daughter. Can your heart endure, or can your hands remain strong, in the days when I shall deal with you? I, the Lord, have spoken, and will do it.*
> (Ezekiel 22:11, 14 NKJV)

Sexuality in the Bible is all kinds of messed up. The man after God's own heart, David, exerts the power of his office over Bathsheba and then kills her husband, various people are married to their half siblings, and women are treated like property rather than granted the dignity God desires for each person. The concept of incest is biblically confusing and even scripturally justifiable for some familial connections, if you are so inclined to walk down that path of justification.

Despite this confusing reality, most Christians recognize incest isn't a good thing, particularly when it is coupled with force or coercion, as it so often is, with an older male as predator and a young, vulnerable person as victim.

Here are two #YouKnowMe stories to illustrate the kinds of incest situations which result in girls showing up at abortion clinic doors.

> *I'm a nurse who assisted with 2nd trimester abortions, mostly in cases of rape and incest. My youngest patient was 11 years. She was raped by her Uncle and came to the hospital with her heartbroken mom. I still have the letter of gratitude that the mom wrote to me. That little 11 year old girl mattered! Her body, her rights, her life mattered!*

> *I refuse to be silent anymore. My silence was out of shame. I had an abortion 30 years ago because of incest. My predator was my own paternal grandfather. Ten years of his misery. It was abortion or suicide. I had to do what was right for me.*

One of the reasons rape and incest go hand-in-hand in the abortion debate is that they frequently occur simultaneously. In these two examples, young girls were raped by family members. They were children themselves, but are expected by many lawmakers to carry the potentially genetically compromised children of their serial abusers.

Today's passage shows us God is not pleased by the abuse it describes. Our God of love is not happy when children are violated by family members, stealing their innocence and changing them forever.

Might God have the empathic nuance to be offended when the violation is continued by forcing the child to carry a baby to term and give birth? Might there be room in God's heart for mercy in these situations?

> *There's a reason they call childbirth labor. Making a healthy baby takes effort: It requires foresight and self-denial and courage. It's expensive and demanding and tiring. You have to learn new things, change many habits, possibly deal with complicated medical situations, make difficult decisions, and undergo stressful ordeals. I had a wisdom tooth pulled without Novocaine while I was pregnant—it hurt a lot and seemed to go on forever. The kindness of the very young dental assistant, holding back my hair as I spat blood into a bowl, will stay with me for the rest of my life. Pregnant women do such things, and much harder things, all the time. For example, they give birth, which is somewhere on the scale between painful and excruciating. Or they have a cesarean, as I did, which is major surgery. None of this is without risk of death or damage or trauma, including psychological trauma. To force girls and women to undergo all this against their will is to annihilate their humanity.*
> Katha Pollitt

Day 20: Domestic Violence

And following Him was a large crowd of the people, and of women who were mourning and lamenting Him. But Jesus turning to them said, "Daughters of Jerusalem, stop weeping for Me, but weep for yourselves and for your children. For behold, the days are coming when they will say, 'Blessed are the barren, and the wombs that never bore, and the breasts that never nursed.' Then they will begin to say to the mountains, 'Fall on us,' and to the hills, 'Cover us.'
(Luke 23:27-30 NASB)

Did you know that the number one cause of maternal death is murder?[5] The National Domestic Violence Hotline website has an entire category titled "Pregnancy and Abuse." Violence against pregnant women is considered a "major public health concern."[6]

Here are a few #YouKnowMe stories about this happening.

I had an abortion when I was 16 to a 22 year old psychopath who beat me regularly. He didn't know. He has openly stated that if his attempts at getting me pregnant had worked he would have taken the child and killed me. If I had that baby, I would be dead.

At the age of 16 i was in a very abuse relationship with a guy who was constantly threating to kill me and my family. he told me if i didn't get an abortion he would do it for me and make sure i didn't have a baby. WHY would i ever want to put a child in that situation

I was 16. I WAS A CHILD. Chose not to terminate but ended the relationship w/ my abusive bf. He chose to BEAT me until the baby died. After basically going through labor and delivering my dead 4 month old fetus had to have a D&C. It was so traumatic.

Young women and socioeconomically disadvantaged women are particularly vulnerable to physical abuse while pregnant. Can you imagine what it must be like to discover you conceived when you

---

[5] Death By Pregnancy: Why Are So Many Moms-To-Be Dying?, Women's Health Magazine, October 2017
[6] Preventing or Reducing Partner Violence Against Women During Pregnancy, The Cochrane Collaboration, November, 2014

know how angry it will make your abusive boyfriend? Or what if you were desperate to escape your relationship but scared you'd be killed? What would it be like to imagine the baby being brought into that environment, even if the man thought he wanted it?

These situations are tragedies; horrible situations in which women wish they were barren, as today's scripture mourns. The desperation and terror they endure is impossible to comprehend for any of us who are not in those situations.

God, on the other hand, knows exactly what they are suffering, and desires their freedom from physical and emotional abuse. So how likely would God be to condemn an abused 16-year-old for their decision to abort?

How should you judge them, in light of that?

> *We are here to awaken from the illusion of our separateness.*
> Thich Nhat Hanh

Day 21: Gender Dysphoria

There is neither Jew nor Greek, there is neither slave nor free, there is no male and female, for you are all one in Christ Jesus.
(Galatians 3:28 ESV)

Not everyone who has an abortion is a women.

If you aren't familiar with gender issues, this may be news to you, however, it's a reality. Intersex and transgender men can have fully functioning female reproductive organs, and can be impregnated. While some of these people have surgical procedures to alter their genitals and internal organs, others do not.

Because of this reality, it's possible for a transgender or intersex man to become pregnant, which can result in intense gender dysphoria: emotional and psychological distress related to their bodies. In some circumstances, men in these situations decide to abort, feeling as if their biology has betrayed them.

I try to imagine how difficult it must be to have lived much of my life masquerading as a woman when I wasn't, only to be faced with something which is so intrinsically and publicly connected to the female sex. I hope you can try to imagine it as well, regardless of how foreign the concept is.

God calls us to empathy. We are called to emulate Jesus in his understanding of all our experience, including gender dysphoria.

I recognize that this may be confusing to you, and that's okay. You don't have to understand it completely. But God does want you to extend compassion.

During the darkest part of the night, when no light seems to exist, just on the other side of the globe is the brightest part of the day. Life is a lot like this. Behind the dark clouds, the sun still shines. Within our greatest challenges and obstacles, exists a beautiful lesson and gift waiting for us. No matter how it may seem to us at the moment, the Creator is always there for us and there is a reason for every path that we take. Remembering that the Light is there, always shining, will make the morning come all the sooner.
Karen Berg

Check Your Privilege

Privilege is the set of circumstances which puts us in a position of not having to face challenges others face. Privilege is like breathing. It's always operating, but we only think about it if a problem arises.

The next few days of reflections focus our attention on areas of privilege which impact our evaluation of the abortion issue. May God open our hearts to be more aware of how our advantages color our judgments.

Day 22: The Privilege of Economic Security

Open thy mouth, judge righteously, and plead the cause of the poor and needy.
(Proverbs 31:9 KJV)

Economic insecurity is an ever-present worry. It gnaws at you, preventing sleep and limiting your ability to enjoy even the simplest pleasures. It's hard enough when you are young and single, trying to scrape up enough money to pay for housing and a case of ramen noodles. It's much, much worse for women who are struggling to provide for the children they currently mother. The worry can be crippling.

Here are a few #YouKnowMe stories to give you a sense of what many people experience:

I had an abortion last year after the tubal ligation I had 8 years ago failed and one of my tubes grew back together. We could not afford a fourth child. The 3 we already have must come first.

I was 22, alone, the birth control failed, the birth father disappeared, I had no money, no health insurance and no clue how I was supposed to give birth to an unwanted child. Thank God abortion was legal & safe.

I gladly gave birth to and loved 6 children. Getting pregnant with a 7th, when I was divorced, broke and in ill health was a nightmare. My abortion was nothing but a relief and I have never, ever regretted it.

My boyfriend broke up with me when he found out I was pregnant. I could barely feed myself or keep a roof over my head on what I made. I had an abortion, no regrets.

I was 22- a condom broke. I was working 2 jobs, no insurance, NO family help- on my own since I was 18. The father wanted nothing to do with a baby- abortion was the only choice.

Perhaps you've been blessed with a good education and a comfortable, middle-class upbringing, and have never dealt with those kinds of fears. But you should recognize these circumstances as privilege, and try to adjust your judgment of others because of it.

Scripture shows us that God has always had a special place in their heart for the poor. Remember this while you consider the women who choose to abort.

Reproductive choice has to be straightened out. There will never be a woman of means without choice anymore. That just seems to me so obvious. The states that changed their abortion laws before Roe are not going to change back. So we have a policy that only affects poor women, and it can never be otherwise.
Ruth Bader Ginsburg

Day 23: The Privilege of Being Able to Say No

Then it happened one evening that David arose from his bed and walked on the roof of the king's house. And from the roof he saw a woman bathing, and the woman was very beautiful to behold. So David sent and inquired about the woman. And someone said, "Is this not Bathsheba, the daughter of Eliam, the wife of Uriah the Hittite?" Then David sent messengers, and took her; and she came to him, and he lay with her, for she was cleansed from her impurity; and she returned to her house. And the woman conceived; so she sent and told David, and said, "I am with child."
(2 Samuel 11:2-5 NKJV)

A shocking number of people's opposition to abortion centers around the idea that women should simply keep their legs together.

The idea reeks both of privilege and of sexual oppression.

Many women are in unhealthy relationships where saying no simply isn't permitted. Purity Culture went a long way in insuring that this is the case; girls are raised to believe their male mates are in charge of all things sexual, that they don't need nor should expect pleasure, and that the man has property rights over their bodies. They are trained to think they are the evil cause of male desire and therefore must satisfy it. This kind of thinking is widespread in the conservative Christian circles which also condemn abortion.

To complicate this situation, girls are also often trained to be accommodating and helpful, which means saying no to nearly anything is hard.

If you weren't raised with this kind of thinking, or with other emotional formation challenges which makes saying no problematic, be grateful. You enjoy a particular form of privilege.

If you are in a healthy relationship in which you can work out ways with your partner to not have intercourse in order to avoid pregnancy (or for any other reason) then this is another form of privilege. It's a form I wish everyone had, because relationships with that kind of communication and give and take are rare, precious, and God-designed.

If you are asexual and don't contend with the sex drive which complicates the lives of the vast majority of humanity, recognize that this is yet *another* sort of privilege in the abortion discussion.

Today's scripture passage tells the story of how a king used his power to take a woman and impregnate her. In that time and place, she would have had very little ability to say no.

Slut-shaming women in crisis-pregnancy situations is unfair, and puts you in the circle of rock-menacing men around the woman Jesus protected from stoning They didn't know her story, and you don't know the stories of the countless women whose pregnancies create desperation.

Not everyone can say no. If you can, consider it a very deep privilege.

The Christian community must be concerned about and address the circumstances that bring a woman to consider abortion as the best available option. Poverty, unjust societal realities, sexism, racism, and inadequate supportive relationships may render a woman virtually powerless to choose freely.
204th General Assembly (1992), Presbyterian Church (U.S.A.)

Day 24: The Privilege of Being a Man

You, then, why do you judge your brother or sister? Or why do you treat them with contempt? For we will all stand before God's judgment seat. It is written:

"As surely as I live,' says the Lord, 'every knee will bow before me; every tongue will acknowledge God."

So then, each of us will give an account of ourselves to God. Therefore let us stop passing judgment on one another. Instead, make up your mind not to put any stumbling block or obstacle in the way of a brother or sister.
(Romans 14:10-13 NIV)

For a number of years I attended a socially conservative church with an all-male clergy and governance structure. During those years I was also very pro-life, and considered myself a single-issue voter. It seemed to me then that men should have rights over the unborn children women carried. While my heart knows there are good men who in many cases *should* have a say over the outcome of a pregnancy, I've swung a long way from my previous view. There are just too many cases where the fathers are significantly problematic: abusive, negligent, or overly controlling. And even though they may have supplied the genetic material which created the child, their lives are often largely unchanged when a baby is born.

In contrast, women's lives are irrevocably impacted. It's like that old saying: the difference between involvement and commitment is like ham and eggs: the chicken is involved, but the pig is committed. In the abortion issue, men might be involved, but women's lives are sometimes sacrificed by pregnancy.

There have been too many decades when men in government have made decisions about abortion, when their own lives will only be tangentially touched by it.

If you are someone whose biology means sex can never result in carrying a child, you have a particular privilege which should impact your participation in the discussion. Please pray about the role God desires for you in this great debate of our age.

Since man's ruling over woman is itself a result of the fall, man must not have ruled over woman before the fall. The practical result of men ruling over women, even in the best of circumstances, is that women are deprived of the corresponding authority with men that God granted them in creation. Furthermore, because of their fallen nature, many men have used their positions of authority to abuse women. Christ, the seed of the woman God promised would crush the serpent's head (Gen 3:15), has overcome the fall. Consequently, we should resist the tragic consequences the fall introduced, including man's rule over woman, not foster them.
Phillip B. Payne

Day 25: The Privilege of Access

When they are diminished and brought low
through oppression, evil, and sorrow,
he pours contempt on princes
and makes them wander in trackless wastes;
but he raises up the needy out of affliction
and makes their families like flocks.
The upright see it and are glad,
and all wickedness shuts its mouth.
Whoever is wise, let him attend to these things;
let them consider the steadfast love of the Lord.
(Psalm 107:39-43 ESV)

Many pro-life advocates focus on forcing clinics to go out of business, assuming that if abortion providers aren't readily available, women won't be able to have their pregnancies terminated. But let's be real for a minute. Are the clinics themselves the problem? Is eliminating them the solution? Will removing providers result in fewer women having crisis pregnancies?

Are abortion clinics the *cause* of unplanned pregnancy? Do those of us who hold pro-life views even care?

Shouldn't we care?

What about the extreme cases? How do we deal with the 11-year-old rape victim who now carries her assailant's child? Is it possible that clinics should continue to exist, if only for the limited number of situations like that one?

These are tough questions, but good ones. Our God wants you to wrestle with them.

The reality is that those who live in states which legislate for open access to abortion, and those who can afford to travel to one of those places, have a particular kind of privilege. If you're one of these people and find yourself or someone you love in a desperate situation, you'll be able to get abortion services.

Not everyone can say the same.

Ultimately abortion takes place because there is something wrong within the culture, within the system, and not simply because this or that particular woman is seeking to end an unwanted pregnancy.
Ronald Rolheiser

Day 26: Check Your Self-Righteousness

Woe to you, scribes and Pharisees, hypocrites! For you tithe mint and dill and cummin, and have neglected the weightier provisions of the law: justice and mercy and faithfulness; but these are the things you should have done without neglecting the others.
(Matthew 23:23NASB)

Our God is above all things and the creator of all things, the force which holds matter together and creates stars and planets from the sheer force of their imagination. They are also the God who loves each of us intimately, and who knows us better than we know ourselves.

This transcendent, immanent God looks upon our unique gifts and joys, and dreams of the life work for which we are a perfect fit. Our Creator desires us to be one with them, with each other, and with creation, and each person's mission should focus on those things.

If you think your mission calls for actions which create harm, there might be something wrong with your understanding of the work. If you believe an end result means the hearts and minds hurt along the way don't matter, you probably have God's will for your life wrong. If your own sense of righteousness fuels your objection to abortion, something is out of kilter.

I understand the yearning to prevent women from taking an action they may deeply regret in future years, and to rescue the tiny beings who may not emerge alive. I've been there. But if in the urgent necessity to "save" these humans from a distance the situation is viewed as an intellectual exercise, you are ignoring the realities of the wounded, and God is not pleased.

We are called to the weightier provisions of the law: mercy and faithfulness. Self-righteousness makes us focus on the lesser things.

Necessity is not the language of faith. It's the language of addition.
Joshua Noah

Day 27: Check Your Hypocrisy

"Stop judging, so that you won't be judged, because the way that you judge others will be the way that you will be judged, and you will be evaluated by the standard with which you evaluate others. Why do you see the speck in your brother's eye but fail to notice the beam in your own eye? Or how can you say to your brother, 'Let me take the speck out of your eye,' when the beam is in your own eye? You hypocrite! First remove the beam from your own eye, and then you will see clearly enough to remove the speck from your brother's eye."
(Matthew 7:1-5 ISV)

Eileen Egan, a Roman Catholic activist and co-founder of several Catholic peace organizations, contemplated the gospel account of Jesus' clothing being divvied up before his crucifixion, and said:

The protection of life is a seamless garment. You can't protect some life and not others.

What it means is that issues like capital punishment, social justice, abortion, militarism, and abortion should all be approached using consistent moral principles. If life is sacred, then it should be dealt with as sacred at all levels. But it's easy to look around the political landscape, or in our families, or even in the mirror and see that many people place a great deal of focus on the life of a multi-week child in the womb while ignoring the sacredness of toddlers kept in cells on the United States southern border, or men on death row.

As mentioned previously, Jesus tells us to let our yes be yes, and our no be no. He said it as a warning to not make vows, but I think his view on this issue would be the same. In today's scripture passage, we hear him warning against both judgment and hypocrisy. If you're willing to let refugees die of hunger, thirst, and illness, or if you support bombs being dropped in other nations, or if you think death by lethal injection is perfectly fine, then you aren't pro-life. You are simply anti-abortion.

And you're a hypocrite.

It must be pointed out that the same society so determined to defend the rights of the fetus shows no interest in children after they are born; instead of trying to reform this scandalous institution called public assistance, society prosecutes abortionists; those responsible for delivering orphans to torturers are left free; society closes its eyes to the horrible tyranny practiced in "reform schools" or in the private homes of child abusers; and while it refuses to accept that the fetus belongs to the mother carrying it, it nevertheless agrees that the child is his parents' thing.
Simone de Beauvoir

Dealing with the Aftermath

Abortion is unlike other medical procedures, and often has a lingering impact. Over the next few days we'll take a look at some issues related to recovery.

Day 28: Regrets

Remember him—before the silver cord is severed,
and the golden bowl is broken;
before the pitcher is shattered at the spring,
and the wheel broken at the well,
and the dust returns to the ground it came from,
and the spirit returns to God who gave it.
(Ecclesiastes 6:6-7 NIV)

As stated in the introduction, I've had two abortions.

The first was when I was 16, around 1979. My parents were in the process of divorcing, and my mom was an emotional wreck. I had to skip school and take a bus an hour away to a Planned Parenthood to confirm I was pregnant. It was the first time I'd skipped school, because I was a good girl. The second time I was 18 or 19, still with the same guy, still just as freaked out and unable to visualize introducing a baby to our unstable relationship.

Abortion was never discussed in my house growing up. I didn't really have an opinion about it. It was just something there if a girl needed it. An unpleasant necessity. We weren't religious, so fears of hell didn't factor into the decisions. But I knew what pregnancy was. I knew babies had been planted, and were growing. I also knew having a child with my boyfriend at those times was just not possible. There weren't any discussions about other options.

It's a rough procedure. There are sights and sounds you don't easily forget. I cried, before, during, and after. But I had no idea that I'd be dealing with regrets 40 years later.

I ended up marrying that boyfriend and over the course of the years we had two more children together. When my youngest child began to turn into a person, morphing from generic infant to inquisitive, focused toddler, I compared these two kids who I adored. As the years passed their differences were amplified, two tines from a single handle arcing off and twisting into arabesques and clever twinings I could never have imagined.

Their differences were fascinating. Compelling. Absorbing. They had the same genetic base, the same nurture, and yet were extraordinarily different. Their magnificent particularity had nothing to do with me other than my "yes". Every bit of who they were was due to the sheer beautiful whimsy of creation itself. A chance coalescing of ingredients into being.

And so I began to mourn. Not for some *Leave it to Beaver* 1950s version of family. I knew what my marriage was like. I recognized the brokenness that I brought into it and my flaws as a mother. I mourned for the world, that two creations as brilliantly colored and exquisitely, particularly, detailed had been stamped out of existence due to my "no."

Hear me now: I don't judge women who feel like they have no other choice than to abort. I understand that feeling, all too well. I felt the panic, the despair, and the pressure. I worked hard to believe that what was being removed from me was just a bit of tissue, a few renegade cells, not that much different from cancer in their ability to disrupt a life. So I don't judge those despairing, cornered girls.

I can only reflect on the stunning particularity of my two living children, and catch my breath in awe and wonder. And I will always mourn not permitting those other two the chance to develop into their own intensely unique and beautiful selfdom.

Not everyone will experience the regret that will be my lifelong companion. But many will. And it's only right and fair to the women considering abortion today to talk about this. They have a right to know.

Regrets are a side effect of abortion.

Between stimulus and response there is a space. In that space lies your freedom and power to choose your response. In those responses lie your growth and your happiness.
Commonly attributed to Viktor Frankl

Day 29: Health Risks

Be sober, be watchful. Your adversary the devil prowls around like a roaring lion, seeking some one to devour. Resist him, firm in your faith, knowing that the same experience of suffering is required of your brotherhood throughout the world. And after you have suffered a little while, the God of all grace, who has called you to his eternal glory in Christ, will himself restore, establish, and strengthen you.
(1Peter 5:8-10 RSV)

One of my biggest concerns about the abortion debate is the lack of discussion about health risks associated with the procedure. Risks range from the psychological to the physical, from depression and substance abuse to breast cancer and occasionally, barrenness. But it's hard to discuss common sense regulation (which we address in the next section), because many people are afraid that talking openly about the risks will undermine access. Because of this, a great deal of conflicting messaging is broadcast, with abortion described as both a serious health issue requiring attention and coverage by insurance, and a minor procedure involving of an insignificant clump of cells.

So let's recognize that health risks do exist, and talk about a couple of them.

Many (not all) women experience abortion as traumatic, and suffer from the repercussions of that trauma for decades. This reality should be addressed up front.

A potential link to breast cancer is hotly debated. Here's an inexpert summary of the connection: in the early stages of pregnancy, breast tissue begins transforming to support the later needs of the infant for nursing. When the pregnancy is artificially halted through abortion, the morphing process is disrupted, leaving those cells vulnerable to cancer. While there haven't been enough studies yet to make the connection conclusive, there's enough evidence that women have a right to know it's a possibility. Women should have the information so that after abortion they can be vigilant in conducting breast exams and getting mammograms.

There are more potential problems, of course. These are just a representative example.

Today's scripture urges us to be watchful, because darkness looms around unexpected corners. Women need to know what they might encounter as a result of having an abortion. They have a right to be watchful. Potential risks and side effects shouldn't get brushed under the carpet just to protect the institution of abortion, any more than they should have been hidden by the tobacco industry.

Without that information, there can be no "right to choose," because women don't know what they are choosing.

A woman's health is her capital.
Harriet Beecher Stowe

Day 30: The Problem of Not Mourning

This is what the LORD says: "A voice is heard in Ramah, lamentation and bitter crying. Rachel is crying, and she refuses to be comforted for her children, because they are no longer alive."
(Jeremiah 31:15 ISV)

It's common to hear mothers who miscarry say people didn't treat their loss as if it was a big deal. They often report they weren't able to mourn.

This attitude is really unhealthy. Someone who loses a child in utero needs to mourn. The child was real, and the loss is real. Grieving is part of healing.

Many (perhaps most) people who abort also need to grieve. But because abortion is such a fraught and shame-filled topic, we aren't given that opportunity. We hide and subsume our grief, pretending the whole thing never happened, at least publicly, pretending the beings forming within us weren't what our hearts knew them to be.

As mentioned early on in this book, some people do intellectually distance what is growing in their bodies from personhood, and for those people, the need is less or in some cases, even non-existent. But for many, grieving is necessary, for the lost potential of the child, for lost motherhood, for lost innocence in having simply endured the experience. A change takes place when a pregnancy is terminated, and it's not an insignificant shift. Removing a growing baby isn't the same as removing a tooth or a near-rupturing appendix. The complexity should not be dismissed.

If you know someone who's experienced abortion, be sensitive to this issue. Give them space and permission to grieve.

How many others suffered in silence, too ashamed and too afraid to speak about their pain? The world wouldn't let them grieve for children they had aborted. How could they when the rhetoric said there was no child? How does one grieve what doesn't exist? No one wanted to admit the truth.
Francine Rivers

Day 31: The Potential for Healing

For I am sure that neither death nor life, nor angels nor rulers, nor things present nor things to come, nor powers, nor height nor depth, nor anything else in all creation, will be able to separate us from the love of God in Christ Jesus our Lord.
(Romans 8:38-39 ESV)

Millions of people walk around carrying abortion wounds, some of them acknowledging the pain, and others subsuming it. These millions are in need of healing. It's hard to heal if we don't deal with those wounds, and it's hard to deal with wounds if we pretend they don't exist.

When we sublimate darkness rather than letting the healing, cleansing light shine in, it's not possible to blossom and prosper. God desires our wholeness, and our freedom. We can't fully love and freely serve when our wounds remain hidden and untreated.

If you've been through abortion but have damped the whole thing down, it might be time to deal with it. You might need to mourn, as we discussed yesterday. You might need the help of supportive clergy, or a counselor, or a trusted friend to talk it all through. You may need to forgive yourself and the others who were involved when it happened.

It's possible you'll have regrets, as I do, but that's a survivable reality. Think about them as scars which remain after a wound has healed. It would be nice if they didn't exist, but they do. And that's part of life. No-one escapes without signs of our struggles.

Please know I am praying for you, right now, through these words. May you be whole, and healed. May you realize your belovedness. May you walk forward into the future unburdened. And may you always remember that nothing can separate you from the love of God.

Dealing with the Aftermath

If you haven't been through abortion but know someone who has, consider acting as the mouth of God and passing these prayers along to them as well.

It has been said, "time heals all wounds." I do not agree. The wounds remain. In time, the mind, protecting its sanity, covers them with scar tissue and the pain lessens. But it is never gone.
Rose Fitzgerald Kennedy

What about Regulation?

Political battles are waged each election cycle with abortion legislation as a key component of candidate and party platforms. In the coming days we'll look at issues related to regulation, so we can prayerfully discern what legislation to support as Christians, if any.

Day 32: Common-Sense Regulation

Remind them to be submissive to rulers and authorities, to be obedient, to be ready for every good work, to speak evil of no one, to avoid quarreling, to be gentle, and to show perfect courtesy toward all people.
(Titus 3:1-2 ESV)

Abortion advocates tend to have a knee-jerk reaction to regulatory measures, viewing them as a slippery slope leading to the dissolution of the procedure's legality. The response is somewhat understandable, because so much legislation is being passed at the state level which seeks to put abortion clinics out of business. These regulations don't seem to be focused on keeping women safe when receiving procedures which have been proclaimed legal by the Supreme Court. Instead, they appear to be trying to make clinics disappear.

Most rational people understand the need for common-sense gun laws. The idea of a complete lack of regulation about something as important as weapons seems laughable. So given the impact on lives which abortion has, shouldn't we view it in a similar light? Shouldn't we be able to accept the sensibleness of regulating procedures which are literally related to life and death?

If we truly value life, then the life of the mother should be just as important as the life of the child. And if we truly value women, we should care about the quality of medical care they receive. Common-sense regulation is needed for both.

The issue of regulation is complicated. Please educate yourself as legislation is considered in your area, and pray about the action our loving God would have you take when communicating with legislators.

The church has a responsibility to provide public witness and to offer guidance, counsel and support to those who make or interpret laws and public policies about abortion and problem pregnancies. Pastors have a duty to counsel with and pray for those who face decisions about problem pregnancies. Congregations have a duty to pray for and support those who face these choices, to offer support for women and families to help make unwanted pregnancies less likely to occur, and to provide practical support for those facing the birth of a child with medical anomalies, birth after rape or incest, or those who face health, economic, or other stresses.
217th General Assembly (2006), Presbyterian Church (U.S.A.)

WHAT ABOUT REGULATION?

DAY 33: FORCED OR COERCED ABORTION

As it is my eager expectation and hope that I will not be at all ashamed, but that with full courage now as always Christ will be honored in my body, whether by life or by death.
(Philippians 1:20 ESV)

In a troubling number of cases, abortion patients are forced or coerced into having them. The young are particularly vulnerable to this, because they are financially dependent on their parents, and can face homelessness or removal from college if they don't terminate their pregnancies. Another scenario is that boyfriends threaten violence if they don't abort. Here's a #YouKnowMe story where this was the case:

> *I was 21, my son was 7 months. His father slammed my head into the car window three times and told me if I didn't get an abortion he would kill me then himself. I did it to save my life and I don't think he would have cared if the procedure was safe or legal.*

Within the last year, news reports divulged that nuns who'd been raped by priests were forced to have abortions, to cover up the scandals which would have arisen if children were born.

None of these scenarios are acceptable. All of them are a kind of raping, with a removal of choice involving reproductive autonomy. Shame is often a driver in these situations.

The pro-choice movement pushes back against legislation which prohibits forced or coerced abortion, fearing the blasted slippery slope. But forced abortions aren't uncommon, and force is the opposite of choice. In these situations, the girls and women aren't able to provide true consent, which means the abortions are unethical health care.

God cannot be pleased when people are coerced and shamed into having abortions. Regulation should be in place to help screen for when it occurs.

> *If men could get pregnant, abortion would be a sacrament.*
> Florynce Kennedy

Day 34: Conscientious Objection

But Daniel resolved that he would not defile himself with the king's food, or with the wine that he drank. Therefore he asked the chief of the eunuchs to allow him not to defile himself.
(Daniel 1:8 ESV)

In today's scripture we hear of Daniel's efforts to remain faithful to his religious tradition regarding consumption of unclean foods. He was an early example of a conscientious objector.

Here in the United States, the concept of religious freedom has come to be equated with the ability of Christians to refuse to bake cakes for gay weddings or for civil servants to refuse to issue marriage licenses. The issue is complex and nuanced, particularly when the services being refused are things related to rights granted by the Supreme Court.

Abortion procedures are one of the things which Christians may determine they simply cannot participate in because of their faith. While it may be a rare situation since most abortions are performed in clinics where people with those beliefs wouldn't seek jobs, procedures do take place in other settings for a variety of reasons.

Even the most adamant of pro-choice advocates should acknowledge the reasonableness of people in health care to refuse to participate in abortion procedures.

Shouldn't conscientious objection rights be seen as a common-sense addition to abortion regulations rather than a threat to abortion access?

What about Regulation?

The argument is, after all, about choice.

So great is the value of a human life, and so inalienable the right to life of an innocent child growing in the mother's womb, that no alleged right to one's own body can justify a decision to terminate that life, which is an end in itself and which can never be considered the "property" of another human being. The family protects human life in all its stages, including its last. Consequently, "those who work in healthcare facilities are reminded of the moral duty of conscientious objection. Similarly, the Church not only feels the urgency to assert the right to a natural death, without aggressive treatment and euthanasia", but likewise firmly rejects the death penalty.
Pope Francis

Day 35: Fetal Age

Yet, you are the one who took me from the womb, and kept me safe on my mother's breasts. I was dependent on you from birth; from my mother's womb you have been my God.
(Psalm 22:9-10 ISV)

While the phrase "late-term" has traditionally been used in OB/GYN circles to describe pregnancy which extends beyond the typical due date, it's frequently used today when referring to abortion taking place in the latter part of the second and into the third trimester. Laws vary from state to state on the fetal age in which abortions are legal, and for what reasons they may be sought. The American College of Obstetricians and Gynecologists report that abortions in these later stages of pregnancy are quite rare, but they do take place. In states which permit them, they are generally limited to cases where the mother's life or health is at risk. Physical problems such as preeclampsia, placental abruption, and placenta accreta are examples of some life-threatening conditions.

Abortion is never a pleasant business, and the later in the pregnancy it occurs, the more ugly and dangerous it becomes. Drugs may be administered to the baby to stop their heart from beating prior to the extraction. In some procedures, the skull of the child is emptied and then crushed to make delivery easier. The child in the womb may have reached viability, meaning the stage of development allows survival after birth under normal circumstances. The process typically takes several days, in which the mother's cervix is chemically dilated, and in some cases, the deceased baby's bones are softened.

Pro-life advocates like to point out the horrors of what I've just described, and it *is* pretty horrible. Pro-choice proponents like to not think about what actually happens, which is understandable. But in order to seek a third way, we have to be honest about what's actually taking place. We can't seek God's will without steeping ourselves in truth.

The truth is that the procedures are horrifying, and hopefully people on both sides of the argument can agree that regulation related to abortion in late stages of pregnancy is logical.

What about Regulation?

A 2019 news story[7] profiled three women who obtained procedures late in their pregnancies. One situation involved risk of death to the mother. Another was due to a severe fetal anomaly. In the third case, the pregnant young woman simply did not want to have a child and give it up for adoption, because her mother had abandoned her at the hospital when she was born. She tried to get an abortion earlier, but a variety of delays pushed the procedure into the third trimester. Each of these cases are sad, each involve different kinds of trauma, and each offer fodder for discussion related to regulation.

We are called to be informed about what is actually happening, and to participate in our legislative process based on that learning. Today's entry may have offered information you didn't previously know, but even if it didn't, your task is to consider this in prayer, and ask God to guide you on what common-sense legislation looks like related to abortion taking place later in pregnancy.

> *There is much debate in this country over abortion. I have always found it puzzling. There are the right-to-lifers who say that abortion is the equivalent of murder. Then there are those who say a woman's right of free choice must be preserved. What has always struck me as odd is that each side is convinced that only it is right, and the other is wrong. I feel they are both wrong. No one should take away another person's right to choose. And no one should kill an unborn infant. Of course I could just as easily say both sides are right, but I won't. It's a paradox that can't be resolved. I think it is better to admit that than pretend there is a resolution.*
> Christopher Pike

---

[7] They had Abortions Late in Their Pregnancies. These Are Their Stories, CNN Health, April 2019

Day 36: Fetal Pain

Take heed that you do not despise one of these little ones, for I say to you that in heaven their angels always see the face of My Father who is in heaven.
(Matthew 18:10 NKJV)

It's natural for us to avoid thoughts of uncomfortable things. We don't like to think about the animals killed to give us cheeseburgers and chicken wings, and we don't like to think about the suffering of child refugees, sex trafficked teenagers, or what actually happens to fetuses during abortion procedures.

The reality is that forming babies don't exit the mother's body intact. The suction or scraping which occurs in an early abortion means that the fetus is cut or torn into bits. Abortions which take place later in pregnancy are similarly gruesome, or worse.

Studies have shown that fetuses in the womb experience pain earlier than previously understood.[8] How are we to grapple with this issue? The pro-life crowd uses this as an additional reason for abortions to be illegal. The pro-choice crowd fights against the idea that this could be true, and tries to avoid thinking or talking about it.

But if we are seeking a third way, where we try to view the issue holistically with compassion for both woman and child, shouldn't we be willing to tackle the reality that the creature in formation is equipped with pain receptors and at some stages of development would, in fact, suffer while being killed?

Shouldn't even the most adamant pro-choice advocates lobby for pain mitigation measures for the small being as it is put to death? Wouldn't our God of love desire that much mercy?

Compassion is the wish to see others free from suffering.
Dalai Lama

---

[8] Fact Sheet: Science of Fetal Pain, Charlotte Lozier Institute, December 2018.

DAY 37: AGE OF CONSENT

What do you think? If a shepherd has a hundred sheep, and one of them has gone astray, does he not leave the ninety-nine on the mountains and go in search of the one that went astray? And if he finds it, truly I tell you, he rejoices over it more than over the ninety-nine that never went astray. So it is not the will of your Father in heaven that one of these little ones should be lost.
(Matthew 18:11-14 NRSVCE)

Anyone who's had a child, knows a child, or has been a child realizes that the decision-making of the young rarely includes an assessment of long-term consequences. Because of this, adults recognize the wisdom of retaining some decision-making authority over the young ones in their care. This can apply to pragmatic choices such as what kinds of foods constitute an appropriate meal and whether or not to vaccinate, and to the more ethereal decisions such as whether or not a child must go to church.

Schools recognize this as well, telling students what courses are mandatory, involving parents in homework policies, and requiring parental approval for participation in field trips. Schools are particularly sensitive to handling of medication. School nurses generally need a permission slip from a parent or guardian before they can administer over-the-counter pain relievers to a child who shows up at their door with a headache or menstrual cramps. Some schools don't even permit kids to carry their epipens with them.

Most adults believe limiting control for a variety of things is logical. Young people seem peculiarly equipped for living life by the seat of their often-ripped pants and dealing with the consequences later. Given this propensity, what lines should we draw for young girls seeking abortion?

State laws vary about whether adults must be notified or give consent for girls under the age of 18, but there doesn't seem to be any minimum age requirement. This implies that in states with no parental involvement needed, as long as child has menstruated (and can therefore conceive) they can get an abortion. An 11-year-old child, who can't get Tylenol from a school nurse, can walk into a clinic and have a surgical procedure.

Remember what we talked about earlier in this book; most abortion decisions aren't made between a woman and her doctor. They're made by a desperate person in a clinic setting, where there is no access to previous medical history or other important data. Particularly for the young.

I hope you can acknowledge that this is inherently problematic. While abortions for the very young are rare, they do occur. But how much better equipped is a 14-year-old than an 11-year-old? And under what circumstances were these minors impregnated? How many youngsters are delivered to abortion clinics by the predators who preyed on their innocence?

Our scripture for today reminds us of the care God has for children. It's our job as Christians to protect the vulnerable. And it's our job as citizens of a nation which ensures the legality of abortion to wrestle with what laws make sense regarding age of consent.

If you believe or don't believe in abortion, what we're called to do is stand on the side of justice and stand with the oppressed, which is what Jesus did. Jesus stood for those who were oppressed and those who were marginalized, and to be Christ-like is to do the exact same thing Jesus did.
Rev. Shanea D. Leonard

Day 38: Sex Selection

On the day you were born your cord was not cut, nor were you washed with water to make you clean, nor were you rubbed with salt or wrapped in cloths. No one looked on you with pity or had compassion enough to do any of these things for you. Rather, you were thrown out into the open field, for on the day you were born you were despised.
(Ezekiel 16:4-5 NIV)

Abortion is sometimes used to end the life of a growing child because it's not the sex desired by the parents. This phenomenon is more frequent in countries where there is a strong preferential bias toward having sons rather than daughters. Babies who are identified by genetic testing as likely having intersex conditions are also being targeted.[9][10]

Some states have laws prohibiting sex-selective abortion, but the organizations which advocate for abortion services, such as the Guttmacher Institute, push back against such legislation, suggesting that the laws place a burden on providers, and stigmatize women from Asian cultures.[11]

Regardless of your view of abortion, can we all agree that ending a pregnancy due to the baby not being the sex you want them to be is wrong?

Do we really have to hold so tight to the idea that any constraints or restrictions on abortion threaten its availability, the way gun lobbyists demand that banning bump stocks and background checks threatens constitutional rights?

---

[9] Professor Morgan Holmes is Pushing for Change for Intersex People, through Research and Activism, Wilfrid Laurier University News Hub, June 2019

[10] Human Rights and Intersex People, Council of Europe Commissioner for Human Rights, April 2015

[11] Abortion Bans in Cases of Sex or Race Selection or Genetic Anomaly, Guttmacher Institute, October 2015

Shouldn't there be a few lines in the sand we can come together to draw?

Possibly, the root of my reaction against abortion is one of self-interest and of self-identification. Aren't there many in this world who see me as less than human because I am a woman? Aren't there people who would deem me to be politically, socially, or ideologically "degenerate" and "undesirable" because of my atheism, bisexuality, desire not to be a mother, pacifism, or other personal characteristics? How can I demand my inclusion in humanity and yet deny humanity to another? What kind of gamble would I be taking if I allowed a dehumanizing custom to persist in my society without questioning it? If I tolerate the redefinition of what is human according to someone's desire for power and control, don't I make myself vulnerable to someone's determination that I am not worthy of the designation "human"?

Kathryn Reed

Day 39: Fetal Tissue

For you formed my inward parts; you knitted me together in my mother's womb. I praise you, for I am fearfully and wonderfully made. Wonderful are your works; my soul knows it very well. My frame was not hidden from you, when I was being made in secret, intricately woven in the depths of the earth. Your eyes saw my unformed substance; in your book were written, every one of them, the days that were formed for me, when as yet there was none of them.
(Psalm 139:13-16 ESV)

A few years ago a series of videos produced by a controversial pro-life organization introduced a new topic to the abortion debate: the sale of aborted fetal tissue.

By the letter of the law, compensation to clinics for fetal tissue is supposed to be purely expense-based. It's similar to the compensation offered for egg donation, with companies aggressively pursuing female college students who are prime candidates due to the youthful abundance of their eggs, and the severity of their financial need. Do a Google search for "donate eggs" and you'll see that women are offered between $8,000 and $12,000 for a single harvest. The term "payment" is rarely used, however, because of regulations about the sale and purchase of such things. Officially, girls are "donating" rather than "selling," and are "compensated" for the donation.

Sale of the organs of aborted babies are handled the same way, and clinics who work with companies which want the tissue for research or other purposes include the income in their budgets. Organs procured include the brain, heart, thymus, and kidneys. The more intact the organ, the higher the price tag. Even eyeballs are passed along for compensation. Some body parts are more useful the closer they come to being fully developed, so tissue from later-term fetuses is in higher demand.

There was a great deal of outcry against the credibility of the videos. However, the company which was featured for purchasing fetal organs later stopped obtaining the tissue from Planned Parenthood according to a statement on their website.[12] And Planned

---

[12] StemExpress Statement Regarding Termination of Activities with

Parenthood itself didn't deny that the practice takes place. They simply argued how the finances worked.

Presumably, medical advancements are being made through the use of the flesh of these unborn humans. Some may view this as one positive outcome of what are generally very sad stories. But it should seem obvious that common-sense regulations should be in place for this practice. Some women want a say in what happens to the remains of the babies they've had to terminate, especially in later stages of pregnancy. Including consent statements as part of the intake process seems reasonable.

Sale of fetal tissue should also be considered by pro-life people when evaluating efforts to roll back abortion law at the Federal level. Women in crisis pregnancies are extremely vulnerable. Pushing abortion underground could mean opening up an unscrupulous market, with back-alley clinics profiting not only from the abortions, but selling body parts to the highest bidders.

Regardless of your position on abortion access, I hope you can see that regulation about tissue harvesting is necessary. Surely as a nation we can acknowledge that attention is needed.

'And Then There Were None' is a network of former abortion clinic workers who are stepping forward to tell our stories about what really happens behind the closed doors of Planned Parenthood and abortion facilities across America. We are stepping forward because our voices deserve to be heard, and America deserves to know the truth.
Abby Johnson

Planned Parenthood, StemExpress, August 2015

Day 40: Safe, Legal, and Rare

So in everything, do to others what you would have them do to you, for this sums up the Law and the Prophets.
(Matthew 7:12 NIV)

Some years back the phrase "safe, legal, and rare" was used to describe what many on the pro-choice side viewed as the optimal situation related to abortion.

When I was steeped in pro-life work, I'd hear about returning to the era of back-alley procedures but I didn't think very deeply about that reality if abortion protections were reversed. If anything, I thought the phrase was overwrought and melodramatic. But the reality is that they were (and are) dangerous. Surgical procedures taking place without any sort of regulation or oversight are prone to problems.

Prohibition had some interesting effects, but one thing it didn't accomplish was to stop people from drinking. They still drank, but the business end of things went underground, creating an organized crime boom characterized by violence and frequently resulting in death. If abortion rights are rescinded, we can expect something similar, though on a smaller scale. Women will die, and the unscrupulous will profit.

One thing the last decade of politics has shown us is the frequency of illicit affairs taking place in the so called hallowed halls of government and church. Social media and technology ratcheted up exposure to what's probably always been there, and we are starting to see just how far the abuse runs in places of power.

What would men actually do if abortion became increasingly less accessible? Are the male politicians who do so much of the legislating really ready for the backlash among their peers? How will they handle it when the truth comes out about the mistresses they pretend don't exist? How about the priests and pastors who've used abortion to whitewash the sepulchers of damage they've inflicted on vulnerable parishioners?

If surgical abortion becomes illegal, the men who don't want to deal with the fruit of their sexual activity will ensure that back alley abortionists are plentiful. An illegal, illicit, and unsafe industry will thrive, with no safeguards. Frightened women who feel they have no other choice will go to them, and some will die.

The men in legislatures and churches won't really care about that. They won't do much about it. After all, they need the service.

Shouldn't our focus go back to "safe, legal, and rare," even for pro-lifers?

Abortion is the ultimate exploitation of women.
Alice Stokes Paul (American suffragist and women's rights activist.)

Our Calling

The abortion debate is unlikely to settle down for quite some time. Women have sought abortion for centuries, and will continue to do so until the world as we know it ends. So what is our calling as Christians, given that abortion will always be a reality?

Day 41: Called to Hope

But we do not want you to be uninformed, brothers, about those who are asleep, that you may not grieve as others do who have no hope. For since we believe that Jesus died and rose again, even so, through Jesus, God will bring with him those who have fallen asleep.
(1 Thessalonians 4:13-14 ESV)

A man who headed a crisis pregnancy center visited my socially conservative church a decade or so ago to give a talk about his organization's work. He said that since unborn babies aren't baptized, they would not end up in heaven, and this idea was what propelled his work. He claimed he couldn't live with the idea of innocent souls being in limbo because of the decisions of their parents.

1 John 4 tells us that God is love. This is no small statement. It doesn't say that God is loving, but that God *is* love. How can any Christian align that reality with the idea that babies would be barred entrance to a mystical state of presence with the divine solely because the human who hosted them determined they could no longer continuing their development? What kind of God is it that would do such a thing? How would that be a manifestation of love?

Now let's consider how God would judge the women described throughout this book, driven to abort the life blooming within them due to desperation of a thousand different varieties. How would the Jesus of the gospels respond to a teenage girl, crying in fear at what her parents would do if they found out she was pregnant? How would he respond to the woman lying in the recovery room after an abortion procedure who is about to go home to her hungry toddlers, not knowing if they'd have enough food the next week? How angry would he be at the husband who pushed to have their nearly fully formed baby aborted so that his beloved wife might live?

As Christians, we are not called to put our hope in the reams of rules and regulations set forth in the scriptures. We are called to put our hope in the person of Jesus Christ, and the radical ways he extended love to those society condemned. We are called to put our hope in a glorious existence beyond what we experience now, when love is fully revealed and we become one with it and each other.

We are called to hope, and to pass that hope along to others. We are called to spread the good news.

> *If a mother is mourning not for what she has lost but for what her dead child has lost, it is a comfort to believe that the child has not lost the end for which it was created.*
> C.S. Lewis

Day 42: Called to Help

But if anyone has the world's goods and sees his brother in need, yet closes his heart against him, how does God's love abide in him? Little children, let us not love in word or talk but in deed and in truth.
(1 John 3:17-18 ESV)

It's easy for grownups to respond to the needs of children. They don't have as much power as big people. They don't have the same kind of autonomy. Jesus counseled his followers to be like children in the simplicity of their faith and trust.

The beloved disciple called the recipients of his letter "little children," even though they were adults. Through that epistle he speaks to a new set of adults today: you and I and all those who struggle with the difficult issue of abortion.

Children are sometimes torn between their desire to be helpful and generous with toys, treats, and favor. God's image within them wants to shine through, but the fear of scarcity or loss is strong.

We big people aren't a whole lot different in that respect. We want to be helpful, but are worried about so many things. We worry about doing the wrong thing, falling out of favor with God, or losing the respect or admiration of others.

John mimics Jesus in today's passage, entreating his followers to open their hearts to the needs and pains of their brothers and sisters in Christ. He warns us that if we close our hearts to the pain of others, God can't really abide within us.

Figuring out how to respond in love when someone you know is in a crisis pregnancy situation can be hard. There is much to juggle in the evaluation of short- and long-term effects. And there is no single "right" solution.

What we *do* know is that we are called to be helpful, and to not close off our hearts based on our own judgments about right and wrong.

> *The first question which the priest and the Levite asked was: "If I stop to help this man, what will happen to me?" But the good Samaritan reversed the question: "If I do not stop to help this man, what will happen to him?"*
> Martin Luther King Jr.

Day 43: Called to Comfort

Blessed be the God and Father of our Lord Jesus, the Messiah! He is our merciful Father and the God of all comfort, who comforts us in all our suffering, so that we may be able to comfort others in all their suffering, as we ourselves are being comforted by God. For as the Messiah's sufferings overflow into us, so also our comfort overflows through the Messiah. If we suffer, it is for your comfort and salvation.
(2 Corinthians 1:3-6 ISV)

A sermon I heard recently suggested that the thing we are called to be harvesters of is not souls for God, but of suffering. That we are to do what Jesus did and does; to stand with those who hurt, and be co-bearers of their pain. The sermon was based on Matthew 9; a chapter filled with various forms of Jesus' compassion. In it, he heals a woman who bled for twelve years, along with men who were paralyzed, blind, and mute. He brings a young girl back from the dead, and extends love and grace to tax collectors and sinners. The final passage in the chapter is this:

When he saw the crowds, he was deeply moved with compassion for them, because they were troubled and helpless, like sheep without a shepherd. Then he told his disciples, "The harvest is vast, but the workers are few. So ask the Lord of the harvest to send out workers into his harvest."
(Matthew 9:36-38 ISV)

Compassion is made up of two root words: *com*, which means with, and *passion*, which refers to the spiritual, emotional, or physical agitation related to suffering. So when we engage in compassion, we aren't feeling sorry for someone, we are entering into the experience of suffering *with* them.

Today's reading tells us that Jesus' sufferings flow into us. One of the ways this occurs is by keeping space with people who hurt in the world around us. Jesus manifests *his* thirst in those who thirst nearby, and hopes you quench it with a cool drink.

Comfort isn't always about saying or doing the right things. With many kinds of distress or grief, words are essentially useless. What we can do is be present; to simply share time and space with the one who is enduring.

In the case of abortion, this can mean being with someone as they process their decision, as they go through the various steps to get the procedure, and then as they walk through the days, months, and years which follow. It can also mean being with parents or other family members who aren't happy with the decisions their loved ones have made, simply listening when they need to talk, and praying when they need silence.

We can be like God in this simple act. Just as the Holy Spirit dwells with us in our heights and plummets, comforting us in silence and praying for us with groans too deep for words, we can also overflow with the Messiah's comfort for others.

We are called to be comforters, not accusers.

Maybe learning to live with the question marks, recognizing that closure does not always occur, is all I really needed to do. I hadn't expected, coming from a world that fights to see life's beginnings in black and white, to be so comforted by a shade of gray.
Peggy Orenstein

Day 44: Called to Heal

We know that all things work for good for those who love God, who are called according to his purpose.
(Romans 8:28 NABRE)

As I've mentioned before, many people treat abortion the way they view the consumption of meat. A pregnancy termination is viewed as a clump of flesh rather than a soul, just as the package of flesh we pick up in the supermarket is disconnected from the very real cow, chicken, or pig which ended its life to nourish ours. This distancing seems helpful, emotionally, but is it?

Indigenous peoples have many methods of honoring the spirits of the plants and animals they consume. Performing rituals like this is a way of making connection, and of acknowledging that they have ended the life of something which contains a spark of the divine in order to ensure their survival. There is deep wisdom in this action. Honoring the reality of the life force is so much healthier than pretending it didn't exist.

Is it possible to both end the life of a child within the womb and still celebrate that life and honor it? I think so.

If you know someone who is struggling with the aftermath of their abortion, consider offering them this concept. Maybe you can even offer them a prayer like this:

Dear God, I give you thanks for the life which grew within me. I thank you for the uniqueness each potential person presents, and the ways in which that person reflects your glory. I honor that being and the loss to the world it now represents. I pray that the energy it encompassed fully experience your joy as it sings along with the morning stars. Please help me to heal from the pain of the choice I had to make, and strengthen me for the work ahead. In the name of our creator, sustainer, and redeemer; amen.

Scripture reminds us that all things work to the good for those who love God. Go and help those who've experienced abortion remember this truth.

We do not have control over many things in life and death but we do have control over the meaning we give it.
Nathalie Himmelrich

Conclusion

If you came to this book hoping for answers, you've discovered by now that it doesn't offer them.

My hope is that you've spent time contemplating abortion a bit differently than before, and that perhaps you're slightly less vehement than when you began. I hope that in discussions you're more open to listening and hearing the heart and pain of others.

If you've been pro-choice, I hope you're willing to face the reality that babies are actually dying and deserve care through the abortion process, that many women do have long-lasting negative repercussions from their decision, and that common-sense legislation is in the best interest of women.

If you've been pro-life, I hope you're willing to face the reality that the life of a woman is just as important as the life of her unborn child, that the situations which lead to abortion are widely varying and complex, and that abortions won't end through legislation.

Contemplative friar and spiritual author Fr. Richard Rohr said this:

> *Mystics are nondual seers. They don't think one side is totally right and the other side is totally wrong. They can see that each side has a part of the truth. When people on either side of any contentious issue cannot love one another, it means they don't have the big message yet.*

Love doesn't look like just one thing. Sometimes love looks like accessing resources for a woman who believes she has no other choice but abort. Sometimes it looks like going with a woman to her

Conclusion

abortion appointment when there's no one else to offer that mercy. Sometimes it looks like intervening when a mother or boyfriend are strong-arming a girl to abort. These can all be actions of love and mercy.

May our God who *is* love equip you for continued engagement with others on this issue. And may you be a source of inspiration for unity in the face of dissension.

www.ingramcontent.com/pod-product-compliance
Lightning Source LLC
Chambersburg PA
CBHW060204050426
42446CB00013B/2982